Produced and Published by Infinite Generations
137 National Plaza, Suite 300
National Harbor, MD 20745
1-(855)-455-0125
www.infinitegenerations.com

Library of Congress Control Number: 2022901645

ISBN:
978-1-953364-25-8 (Paperback)
978-1-953364-27-2 (Hardback)
978-1-953364-26-5 (E-book)

Printed in the United States of America
First Printing, 2022
Edited by: India Spruill Howard

Photography from Canva

Copyright © 2021 Rev. Dr. Carrie M. Spruill

All rights reserved.
No part of this publication may be reproduced, distributed, or transmitted in any form or by any means, including photocopying, recording, or other electronic or mechanical methods, without the prior written permission of the publisher, except in the case of brief quotations embodied in critical reviews and certain other noncommercial uses permitted by copyright law. Unless otherwise noted, all Scripture marked with quotations are from the Holy Bible, King James Version Copyright © 2016 by Thomas Nelson, a division of HarperCollins Christian Publishing, Inc. Used by Permission.

For permission requests, write to the publisher, addressed "Attention: Permissions Coordinator," at the address above.

SUNDAY
INSPIRATIONAL ANOINTING
MESSAGES
Faith | Healing | Hope

Rev. Dr. Carrie M. Spruill

 **Infinite Generations Publishing**

Introduction
A Heavenly Supply Assured By the Cross

The Holy Spirit has inspired me to share the messages in this book with His people. It is important to know that we have a heavenly supply of anointing assured by the Cross. Jesus paid the price for us on Calvary's Cross. Before the Cross, Jesus walked this earth for thirty-three long years, healing all different kinds of sickness. (John 14:12) Jesus said we would do greater works than He did while here on earth. Jesus also said He would send us a helper which is the Holy Spirit to guide and instruct us in doing these works. Believing His Word without a doubt through faith and trust, He will empower you with the Holy Spirit. The power of the Holy Spirit living within enables us to heal all kinds of pain and suffering which affect humanity.

Sometimes God's people do not receive the healing promised to them because of their doubt in taking God at His Word. (Isaiah 55:11) He says, His Word will not return unto Him void. (John 14:13) Whatever you ask in His name, you shall receive. If it is healing you need, you will be healed. Reading and meditating on His Word daily will bring you closer to Him. His presence, which is the Holy Spirit becomes more real as your doubts become less and faith grows.

The presence of the Holy Spirit makes healing available to us through prayer, faith, fasting, and scriptures, which is the Word of God. It is wonderful to know that you have in your possession the power of the Holy Spirit that will heal all your needs and sickness. The scriptures and messages in this book address the empowerment of the Holy Spirit's anointing, which is our helper through **Faith, Healing,** and **Hope.**

Acknowledgements

This book would not have been possible without the extraordinary people who strongly support me.

First of all, my husband, Elijah, showed patience and understanding while I was writing the book. Thanks to my daughter, India, who helped organize and edit the book. She also believes this book will spiritually benefit many people.

Of course, none of this would have been possible without the full support of Infinite Generations Publishers. The team showed faith in helping pull this book together, and I am grateful to them.

Finally, I want to thank all the people who will take the time to read and share this book with others.

Contents

Introduction..................................I
Acknowledgements........................II

Faith

Knowledge Is Power 12
God Is For Us 14
The Word Of God 16
Keep The Faith 18
Created For A Divine Purpose...............20
Hear My Words O Lord........................22
God Is Spirit.......................................24
God Gave Us All Gifts..........................26
Thanking and Praising God In Advance....28
The Road To Bethlehem........................30
Rescue...32
Expect Something To Happen................34
Call Today..36

Healing

True Healing......................................42
The Power of Intercessory Prayer...........44
Pray For Governing Leaders..................46
Pray For The Healing Of Our Nation......48
Pray For All People..............................50
Healing Comes Through Faith...............52
God's Anointing Power........................54
Ultimate Healing Power.......................56

Hope

The Light...62
The Way, Truth And Life Lives On.........64
Breathe New Life.................................66
Faith And Hope Working Together........68
Rejoice With Hope...............................70
Finding Hope In A Troubled World.......72
Up Ahead..74
Light At The End Of The Tunnel...........76

Faith

Knowledge Is Power

"And when the men of that place had knowledge of him, they sent out into all the country round about, and brought unto him all that were diseased."

Matthew 14:35

Reading the Word daily helps us to build a close relationship with our Heavenly Father. When we have knowledge of who He is to us, our lives are complete. This is the presence of the Holy Spirit working within, and at this moment, you have entered into perfect peace through Jesus Christ. Believing and trusting in Him, all diseases are wiped away.

God Is For Us

"What shall we then say to these things? If God is for us, who can be against us?"

Roman 8:31

Scripture tells us God is for us. Through faith and believing, He will empower us to stand up against anything that comes our way.

The Word of God

The Word of God is full of living power. If we meditate on the Word of God, carry it in our hearts, and live by faith, then we will see that all things are possible through Him!

"For the word of God is quick, and powerful, and sharper than any twoedged sword, piercing even to the dividing asunder of soul and spirit, and of the joints and marrow, and is a discerner of the thoughts and intents of the heart."

Hebrews 4:12

Keep The Faith

As we continue to trust in our Lord and Savior during times of unrest, He will continue to walk with us.

So keep the faith because our faithful Savior, who was born on Christmas Day, is right by our side all the way!

"Hitherto hath the Lord helped us."

1 Samuel 7:12

Created For A Divine Purpose

"I will cry unto God most high; unto God that performeth all things for me."

Psalm 57:2

God has a purpose for all of us to fulfill while we journey this land here on earth.

Jeremiah 1:5 tells us our purpose in life was mapped out before we were born.

Through prayer and meditating on the Word of God through faith in Jesus Christ, our purpose will be revealed to us. Once our purpose is revealed, He will anoint us with the Holy Spirit to carry out His purpose.

Philippians 4:13 says, "I can do all things through Christ which strengtheneth me."

Hear My Words O Lord

"Give ear to my words, O Lord, consider my meditation. Hearken unto the voice of my cry, my King, and my God: for unto thee will I pray. My voice shalt thou hear in the morning, O Lord; in the morning will I direct my prayer unto thee, and will look up."

Psalm 5:1-3

Let us wake up each morning meditating on the Word of God. As we start our daily journey, we should first make our prayer requests known unto Him.

Giving thanks unto Him in advance for answering our prayer request, knowing that He has heard our voice. Amen!

God Is Spirit

"For to be carnally minded is death; but to be spiritually minded is life and peace"

Roman 8:6

The Word tells us to let go of the carnal man's way of thinking and let the Spirit control our thoughts according to the Word of God. Therefore, we will live a positive life, full of longevity and peace.

John 4:24 says, "God is a Spirit: and they that worship him must worship him in spirit and truth."

God Gave Us All Gifts

"Now there are diversities of gifts, but the same Spirit. And there are differences of adminstrations, but the same Lord. And there are diversities of operations, but it is the same God which worketh all in all. But the manifestation of the Spirit is given to every man to profit withal."

1 Corinthians 12:4-7

God gave us all gifts for His purpose. Joseph's gift was interpreting dreams. God used Joseph to preserve his family, which would become Israel.

Genesis 41: 17-36, Pharaoh had two dreams. The first one was while standing on the bank of the Nile River, there came seven fat sleek cows, and after them came seven scrawny lean cows. The seven scrawny lean cows ate up the seven fat sleek cows.

Pharaoh's second dream was about a big healthy stalk of wheat and a bad stalk of wheat. The bad stalk swallowed up the good stalk. Joseph's interpretation of the dream was that there would be seven years of severe famine in the land. Therefore, Pharaoh should store up enough food to last for seven years so the country would not be ruined and save the people.

We all have a divine purpose in life, and God wants us to use these gifts to bless and save humanity, just as Joseph did according to the Word!

Thanking and Praising God In Advance

Let us go to God with everything by prayer and supplication in the Spirit. Thanking and praising Him, knowing that our request has been answered.

"Be careful for nothing; but in every thing by prayer and supplication with thanksgiving let your requests be made known unto God."

Philippians 4:6

The Road to Bethlehem

"And it came to pass in those days, that there went out a decree from Caesar Augustus that all the world should be taxed."

Luke 2:1

Under the law, Joseph was in a situation where he must travel back to his hometown, Bethlehem, to be counted in the census. Although, Mary was pregnant, which made traveling almost impossible. In life, we all have a road to travel, and sometimes the circumstances in our path seem to be unbearable.

The angels had already spoken to Joseph and Mary; therefore, they knew their faith in God was with them. The child Mary was carrying was the Son of God!

Whatever comes before us as we journey this land (good or bad), rest assured that our Father in Heaven is traveling on the same road with us.

IT'S GONNA BE ALRIGHT. Amen!

Rescue

"And call upon me in the day of trouble: I will deliver thee, and thou shalt glorify me."

Psalm 50:15

Take all your burdens to God in prayer and praise His name. Because the minute you pray and believe through faith, your prayer has been answered. Amen!

Expect Something to Happen

"And the whole multitude sought to touch him; for there went virtue out of him, and healed them all."

Luke 6:19

While touching the garment of Jesus caused a multitude of people to be healed. The crowd went there "EXPECTING" something to happen, and by touching His garment, healing took place immediately. By "FAITH" they "EXPECTED" and "RECEIVED A HEALING." Scripture says they felt the virtue when it came out of Him. Virtue is the anointing of Jesus' healing power without measure.

Call Today

"Call unto me, and I will answer thee and shew thee great and mighty things, which thou knoweth not"

Jeremiah 33:3

Give God a call today; He will answer. He will tell you things you do not know and what you need to know. He has given us His Word. We just need to listen.

If you have a problem understanding the answer, pray and ask the Holy Spirit to discern the answer for you. Amen!

WRITE DOWN WHAT YOU NEED AND MAKE YOUR REQUEST KNOWN UNTO GOD:

_____
_____
_____
_____
_____
_____
_____
_____
_____
_____
_____
_____
_____
_____
_____

SAY, HEAVENLY FATHER, YOUR WORD SAYS, IF WE HAVE FAITH AND BELIEVE, WE SHALL RECEIVE. TODAY, RIGHT NOW, I AM BELIEVING MY CIRCUMSTANCES ARE HEALED. AMEN!

Healing

True Healing

"Heal me, O Lord, and I shall be healed; save me, and I will be saved: for thou art my praise."

Jeremiah 17:14

There are many different areas in our lives where healing is needed. This scripture talks about healing from sin. This type of healing is where we confess our sins. The Holy Spirit living within has caused a change to take place. Now we are a new person in Christ, and our old ways have passed away. We have a renewing of the mind for the better.

The Power of Intercessory Prayer

"I exhort therefore, that, first of all, supplications, prayers, intercessions, and giving of thanks, be made for all men."

1 Timothy 2:1

Scripture urges us to intercede in prayer for ourselves or others. This is one of the most effective ways of praying. Let us include intercessory prayer in our daily lives. When we pray for others, we take their needs and make them our own by lifting them up in prayer. Believing and having faith in Jesus Christ, God will make a difference in our lives, as well as someone else's life.

Today, pray that the Lord will guide your heart to intercede in prayer, whether it be for you, on behalf of someone else, or on world affairs. Thanking our Heavenly Father in advance, knowing that He has answered your prayer.

Pray For Governing Leaders

Let us all pray for the healing of the world.

Scripture tells us to pray for kings and all others who are in authority, so that we may live a quiet and peaceful life with good conduct.

(1 Timothy 2:2)

Pray For The Healing of A Nation

"*For we walk by faith, not by sight.*"
2 Corinthians 5:7

Help us NOT to look at our circumstances with the naked eye, which may affect our mental and physical health, and cause us to become weary. Prayer through faith helps us to stay strong, so we may do the RIGHT THING, according to your Word. Lord spread your SPIRIT over this LAND for FAITH, PROTECTION, and WISDOM.

Heavenly Father,

We realize that our prayers are the communication line to you who gives us strength through faith to stay positive and strong, so we may not become weary.

Father, we are praying for our nation today. Scripture (1 Timothy 2:2) tells us to pray for the ones in authority over us. Lord, help us to keep our leaders, and each other lifted up in prayer and do according to your Word.

Heal this LAND, so we may come together and build a stronger Nation. Father, you are the ANSWER.

"I will therefore that men pray every where, lifting up holy hands, without wrath and doubting"

1 Timothy 2:8

The Word tells us to pray for all people, as well as the ones in authority over us. Through praying in faith and believing, God will work out all situations. He is pleased when we take the time to lift others up in prayer.

Healing Comes Through Faith

"And Jesus went about all Galilee, teaching in their synagogues, and preaching the gospel of the kingdom, and healing all manner of sickness and all manner of diseases among the people."

Matthew 4:23

Huge crowds followed Jesus expecting a change to take place in their lives. They had heard about a man called Jesus preaching the Word and healing all kinds of sickness. People wanted to know about this man and what He used to heal people. Jesus preached on believing and having faith; all we need is just a little faith to be healed!

God's Anointing Power

"Is any among you sick? let him call the elders of the church; and let them pray over him, anointing him with oil in the name of the Lord."

James 5:14

The Word says to call for the elders of the church to pray and anoint the sick with oil in the name of Jesus. Believing and having faith will bring forth healing. God has empowered them with the anointing.

Ultimate Healing Power

" For he had healed many; insomuch that hey pressed upon him for to touch him, as many as had plagues."

Mark 3:10

Jesus had the power to heal every kind of plague and all manner of illness. This same power is given to us. The Word says many plagues were healed when the people pressed upon him to touch Him. They touched Him because they believed and had faith, and faith brings forth healing.

WRITE DOWN WHAT YOU NEED AND MAKE YOUR REQUEST KNOWN UNTO GOD:

_____

_____

_____

_____

_____

_____

_____

_____

_____

_____

_____

_____

_____

_____

SAY, HEAVENLY FATHER, YOUR WORD SAYS, IF WE HAVE FAITH AND BELIEVE, WE SHALL RECEIVE. TODAY, RIGHT NOW, I AM BELIEVING MY CIRCUMSTANCES ARE HEALED. AMEN!

Hope

The Light

"For thou art my lamp, O, Lord: and the Lord will ligthen my darkness."

2 Samuel 22:29

During this time of unrest due to the pandemic, there has been a lot of pain and sorrow, but the presence of God continues to keep us.

When our situation seems dark, He is the light that brightens our day and makes everything alright!

The Way, Truth, and Life Lives On

"Jesus saith unto him, I am the way, and the truth, and the life: no man cometh unto the Father, but by me"

John 14:6

On the day of His trial, TRUTH stood before Pontius Pilate, knowing that the final verdict of His trial would be death. Only through His death on the cross and rising again on the third day would the penalty for our sins be paid.

Breathe New Life

"Thou wilt shew me the path of life: in thy presence is fullness of joy; at thy right hand there are pleasures for evermore."

Psalm 16:11

As we journey through times of unrest, breathe new life. This comes by putting your trust in God to guide your path. When life circumstances turn to depression, pray to our Heavenly Father afresh as you take a walk with Him on that path. Then you will feel His presence where there is fullness of joy. He says, "At His right hand, there are pleasures forevermore."

Faith and Hope Working Together

"Now faith is the substance of things hoped for, the evidence of things not seen."

Hebrews 11: 1

The Word tells us that having faith is what changes the things hoped for in our circumstances.

With faith and hope working together, you will receive the evidence of your prayers being answered.

Rejoice with Hope

"Rejoying in hope, patient in tribulation; continuing instant prayer."

Romans 12:12

Yes, you can rejoice victoriously while hoping for a better day because the Holy Spirit lives within. This is done by being patient and trusting God while going through your trials and tribulations. Continue to pray daily and expect your situation to change. Rejoice and hope for a better day!

Finding Hope In A Troubled World

"For his anger endureth but a moment; in his favour is life: weeping may endure for a night, but joy cometh in the morning."

Psalm 30:5

> "Be of good courage, and he shall strengthen your heart, all ye that hope in the Lord."
>
> *Psalm 31:24*

As we see today, in a troubled world, when everything seems to be in disarray, scripture tells us to be strong.

For our faith, hope, and salvation are in Christ; therefore, we should not become discouraged and give up.

Our Lord has promised that He will keep our feet from being snared. He wants us to stay strong and trust in God's promise through faith in Jesus Christ.

Up Ahead

"Brethren, I count not myself to have apprehended: but this one thing I do, forgetting those things which are behind, and reaching forth unto those things which are before"

Philippians 3:13

Let us pray for each other as we travel this road with one another. We are all striving for a better day, the Lord is our guide, and He will give us the strength to continue on our way.

Amen!

Light At The End Of The Tunnel

A time to heal.
(Ecclesiastes 3:3)

Give thanks to our Lord and Savior for answering our prayers; we now have treatments for the coronavirus.

Scripture tells us there is a time for healing; this is our season. Let us keep the faith, knowing that our Savior has brought us this far.

He is the light at the end of the tunnel and will see us safely through. Amen!

WRITE DOWN WHAT YOU NEED AND MAKE YOUR REQUEST KNOWN UNTO GOD:

_____
_____
_____
_____
_____
_____
_____
_____
_____
_____
_____
_____
_____
_____

SAY, HEAVENLY FATHER, YOUR WORD SAYS, IF WE HAVE FAITH AND BELIEVE, WE SHALL RECEIVE. TODAY, RIGHT NOW, I AM BELIEVING MY CIRCUMSTANCES ARE HEALED. AMEN!

More from Faith Word Healing

Positive Living Longevity Magazines

A faith-based magazine designed to promote postive living and strengthen your faith!

Available at
Infinitegenerations.com/shop

For more readings to empower your life, check out Faith Word Healing on our website
www.faithwordhealing.org

About The Author

Rev. Dr. Carrie M. Spruill is the Founder of Faith Word Healing Ministries and Faith Word Healing Magazine. She is a true believer in (Jeremiah 1:5) which tells us that God mapped out our purpose in life before being born.

The presence of the Holy Spirit's gifts to teach and heal the sick by laying on of hands was recognized in her life at an early age. By the age of twelve, she taught adult Sunday school classes in church. She gave her first public speaking after being appointed to attend a Baptist Convention at the age of sixteen.

She is an advocate for both spiritual and secular education. Over the years, she has gained extensive knowledge in biblical studies and holds a doctoral degree, master's degree, and several bachelor's degrees. The knowledge she has gained, both spiritual and secular, is used to help others succeed and achieve their God-given purpose in life.

www.ingramcontent.com/pod-product-compliance
Lightning Source LLC
Chambersburg PA
CBHW05085824O426
43673CB00009B/282